To Eat Or Not To Eat?

The Grains Group - Food Pyramid

(2nd Grade Science Series)

Speedy Publishing LLC
40 E. Main St. #1156
Newark, DE 19711
www.speedypublishing.com

Any food made from wheat, rice, oats, cornmeal, barley or another cereal grain is a GRAIN product.

Foods in this group are a source of carbohydrate which provides energy and dietary fibre, helping to keep your bowels healthy and regular.

There are two types of grain products: Whole Grain and Refined Grain.

WHOLE GRAINS contain the entire grain kernel. Some examples on the next pages.

WHOLE-WHEAT FLOUR

OATMEAL

WHOLE CORNMEAL

BROWN RICE

REFINED GRAINS have been milled. Some examples on the next pages.

WHITE FLOUR

WHITE BREAD

WHITE RICE

PASTA

TORTILLAS

CEREALS

www.ingramcontent.com/pod-product-compliance
Lightning Source LLC
LaVergne TN
LVHW060516170826
845677LV00026B/1772

* 9 7 9 8 8 6 9 4 5 0 4 9 4 *